Taught by Life

To: Jonnie Diconner
All the Best
Roosevelt Green
2015

Taught by Life
Art and Stories

Roosevelt Lewis, Jr.

Court Street Press

TAUGHT BY LIFE: ART AND STORIES by Roosevelt Lewis, Jr.

© 2015 Roosevelt Lewis, Jr.

ISBN 978-0-9647444-6-2

Book design: Leslie Wall, Lumpfish Design
Book layout and additional design: Sara L. Chapman, Art Squad Graphics

Cover image: Artries, by Roosevelt Lewis, Jr.
Photographers: Jarred Hamilton and Lisa Brown
Artwork photograph production: Al Doggett Studio
Back cover photograph of Cane River: Jarred Hamilton
Back cover photograph of Roosevelt Lewis, Jr.: Lisa Brown

Editor: Judith Yarrow

Court Street Press
3707 37th Avenue South
Seattle, Washington 98144-7110
courtstreetpress.com

Printed by Bang Printing, bangprinting.com

Printed in the United States of America

10   9   8   7   6   5   4   3   2   1

This book is dedicated to my wife for her support in all my life endeavors, throughout our many years together.

Oak tree, Natchitoches, Louisiana

Let us be taught by life to endure and to continue to work through all the challenges that we may encounter. And when our long years of struggle are finally met with success and abundance, let us remember that success is not determined by those who love the results of our labor, but by God who loves us universally.

Roosevelt Lewis

Contents

Foreword

How I got over

How I got over

You know my soul looks back and wonders

How I got over

— Clara Ward

History makes its mark beyond print and text. It is loud and silently present in the movements and utterances of people who, as the brilliant novelist Richard Wright says, "respond to the warmth of other suns and, perhaps bloom." Wright was lyrically referring to what history has called the great migration of African Americans from the south to the north of the USA.

In his book, *Taught by Life: Art and Stories,* Roosevelt Lewis allows us to stay in the south for a while to discover, imagine, and remember, as the gospel song says, "how we got over." We travel with him—through canvas, paper, wood, and color designed to remind, move, transplant, and recreate—finding Black Cajun Creole roots.

I met Roosevelt decades ago, when we were both members of The Choreopoets, a local theater group in Seattle. I remember when he read his poem, "Black Pearl," offering it as a performance piece for the group. Reading that poem today, I hear the melody he conjured from growing up in Natchitoches, Louisiana, and listening to the Cane River.

Roosevelt's paintings and sculptures are stories that move us to other suns to embrace and bear witness. The brush strokes in his paintings breathe life into our historical past and the present horror, joy, and possibilities in our contemporary lives. Roosevelt's carving of hard surfaces are made pliable, rough, smooth, and alive, in sculptures that beckon us to linger, pause, reflect, and find weight and weightlessness in our abilities to touch, resist, imagine, hold, and let go.

Roosevelt paints, sculpts, and writes poetry and plays that shape footprints, shadows, scenes, and intergenerational embraces and hopes. His works move along the Cane River in Central Louisiana and bloom in places that once seemed strange but, because of the magic of Roosevelt's art, become familiar to all of us.

— Gilda L. Sheppard, PhD, Seattle, Washington, 2014

Roosevelt and Pat Lewis, 2013   *Photograph by Lisa Brown*

Acknowledgments

The forty-eight paintings and sculptures in *Taught by Life: Art and Stories* are inspired by my indelible memories of my birthplace, the Cane River region of Central Louisiana.

As a native son who worked the red dirt where cotton and corn once grew, it is my wish that these art works and stories that examine the social and cultural history of Cane River offer the people of Seattle and the Pacific Northwest and throughout our country, an opportunity to engage deeply with the people and the history of Cane River.

I must first extend thanks to my wife, Patricia Lewis, whom I love dearly and deeply appreciate for her inspiration and technical support over the many years it took to turn my vision for a book into the reality you hold in your hand. Without her, this book would not have been published.

It is my great pleasure also to give special thanks to Marita Dingus, a prolific artist who visited my studio a quarter century ago and believed in my work and was responsible for igniting my art career in Seattle.

I want to thank Al Doggett Studio, which provided high quality photos of my art. Many thanks to my editor, Judith Yarrow, for her belief in my vision, her gracious guidance in revising the stories, and her support at every step in the production of this book. Heartfelt thanks go to Sara Chapman for her creativity in designing and laying out the book, and her patience in guiding me through its many revisions. Many thanks also to McAlister Merchant, Jr. for his review of the book, and to Dr. Tawna Pettiford-Wates for her beautiful Afterword.

I would also like to thank Jerry Large, columnist for *The Seattle Times*, for writing my biography. Dr. Gilda Sheppard's support in this project was invaluable and was very important in the formation of this book. I give a special thanks to Martha Henry of Martha Henry Fine Arts, Inc., in New York for her dedication to this project.

I can't say enough positive things about the people of Jackson Square where I grew up. Listening to their stories and observing their struggles planted the seed that grew into this book.

Finally, it is a great pleasure to acknowledge my family. My father, Roosevelt Lewis, Sr., was a gifted wood carver in his own right. The generous assistance of his old friends who told me stories about him were very important to this book's completion. I want to acknowledge my godfather, Alexandria Dixon, who was in my life when it was most important for a fatherless young boy who needed to be guided through the segregated South. Special thanks are extended to the African American people with whom I hung out on street corners. They, too, helped me survive my journey in life and, ultimately, allowed their lessons to become a part of this book.

Roosevelt Lewis in his studio, 2012   Photograph by Lisa Brown

Introduction

by Martha V. Henry, Martha Henry Fine Arts, Inc., New York

Roosevelt Lewis is one of those rare artists, an autodidact whose talent encompasses both the visual and the literary arts. His subject: his boyhood memories of growing up in the unique, mixed-race communities along the Cane River in Natchitoches, Louisiana, during the mid-20th century when Jim Crow laws ruled. Lewis's paintings, sculptures and stories are deep-rooted reminiscent descriptions of the daily struggle that African Americans endured simply to survive and to prepare the next generation—a struggle matched by their determination to overcome adversity and to find joy as they marched from oppression toward freedom. Recounting the stories of what people did in Cane River when he was a boy, the artist pays close attention to the ordinary details of daily living and uncovers the emotional truth in their lives.

To fully appreciate Roosevelt Lewis and his exceptional art, the viewer must be aware of the history of the artist's birthplace in the three-hundred-year-old African American community of Cane River. An isolated region stretching nineteen miles along Cane River in Central Louisiana, it was founded by French Catholic planters (unlike other southern communities), and its heyday was in the 1800s. A close-knit and complex hierarchical society evolved where Creoles, the white, French-speaking descendants of the early French settlers, created families on the side with blacks, raising them above their lower class French-speaking Cajun cousins. Free people of color were able to accumulate wealth and land and became slave owners like their white neighbors. It was a complicated coexistence that defied some stereotypes.

Lewis was born into a family of sharecroppers and grew up in the early 1950s. He did not receive a formal art education; nevertheless, his artistic sensibility developed at a young age through chance encounters with art. He saw his first master paintings in art history books in the houses where his godmother worked.

As a child, Lewis taught himself to paint and sculpt from materials he scavenged from a garbage dump. Like many self-taught artists, he did not realize he was making art until others told him.

Lewis left Natchitoches when he joined the Army in the late 1960s. He was stationed in Europe where he saw Western and African tribal art for the first time. Henri Matisse and narrative African art would later influence him. When Lewis returned to the U.S., he studied graphic arts and began to develop his artistic discipline and focus.

Seeking opportunities, he became part of the Black Migration from the rural South to the urban centers of the North. Lewis settled in Seattle, Washington, and devoted himself to his various artistic practices. Seattle was also the home of Jacob Lawrence and Gwendolyn Knight, participants in the local art scene. Lewis met Lawrence in the early 1990s and was impressed by their shared commitment to paint the truth about the communities they came from. Today Roosevelt Lewis is a kind of Renaissance man; in addition to being an artist and writer, he is a poet, an actor, a teacher, and a community activist. By serving as a teacher and a community activist, Lewis is fulfilling his duty to prepare the next generation for success and survival by instilling discipline and self-control, values he learned from his Cane River ancestors.

Lewis has settled comfortably into playing an active and leading role in the Seattle arts community, yet the memories of Cane River haunt him and infuse every art object he makes. The stories lived by generations of his family and of his neighbors are distilled in his portrayals of labor (farmers, laundresses, house painters) and relaxation (dancing, drinking, and conversation). Conveyed in an individual style of flattened forms, silhouetted figures, and arbitrary combinations of bright color and space, Lewis aligns himself with his early influence, Matisse, and his artistic comrade, Lawrence. Like Lawrence did in his Great Migration series, Lewis found a way to tell his story of American history with pictorial means, balancing beauty between form and content. Unlike Lawrence however, Lewis portrays the Cane River residents who did not dream of leaving their home, stating that "living among people who had all of their dreams buried with them is why I choose to paint about their lives."

Roosevelt Lewis works in a conscious folk art style that also connects him to William H. Johnson and Romare Bearden. Including Jacob Lawrence, these artists are African American masters who practiced a faux folk aesthetic to better tell their great stories of the African American experience in the 20th century. Johnson, who painted poignant scenes of African American daily life, combined tradition with primitivism to express a spiritual essence in his rural subjects that is akin to Lewis's Cane River stories. Bearden celebrated his childhood memories of rural life in Mecklenburg County, North Carolina, by using a variety of mediums, styles and modalities, as Lewis has done in preserving his childhood memories of the people who lived along Cane River. Lewis shares with Lawrence, Johnson, and Bearden the creation of visual bodies of work that document American history during periods of great struggle when the challenge was to find hope.

Although the Cane River series is an African American story about overcoming the harsh realities of racism, the struggle to reclaim life's joy is a universal theme common to all humanity, and therein lies its appeal. The series forms a collective narrative of resilience and strength expressed in vivid details that Lewis's gift as an artist and storyteller brings to life. The stories of Cane River will haunt you as they have Lewis who was compelled to make them into art. Enjoy the journey to Roosevelt Lewis's Cane River; it promises to be an unforgettable experience.

Biography of Roosevelt Lewis

by Jerry Large, columnist for *The Seattle Times*

Roosevelt Lewis once wanted to be a mortician; instead he became an artist whose work keeps alive the people and culture of the small community beside the Cane River in Natchitoches, Louisiana, where he grew up. His life has been full of struggles, and those too, shape his work. Today he is a survivor and a creator.

Lewis is a painter, a sculptor, and a writer. His art is influenced by the African art he saw in French museums when he was in the army, but the subjects are from the Louisiana of his youth, in works like *Freddie's Place, The Moment,* or *Mother Holding Baby.* But any description of Lewis has to start with the town of Natchitoches and how he fit into it.

Natchitoches has been a cultural mixing place throughout its long history—French, Spanish, American, Creole, Indian, African—the kind of place that brews creativity. Lewis said that if any of the plays he writes ever won a major award, he'd thank the people of Natchitoches, the ones who sat on the one corner where everybody, drunks and highly educated people alike, came together, and where people schooled him on life. "I was always involved with the elders," Roosevelt said. "I always appreciated the knowledge the black men and women shared with me. They all show up in my art." Roosevelt called the Natchitoches of his youth a little segregated town with a lot of good going on in it. "We had our own black grocery stores, service stations."

Roosevelt grew up next to the cemetery. His father was killed when Lewis was seven. His mother was deaf and an alcoholic. She loved books, a love that she passed on to Roosevelt whose job it was to read to her. She couldn't hear, but she would read his lips. "I would get tired sometimes, but she was insistent," he said. Her own formal education had ended at fourteen when she was pregnant with Roosevelt's older brother.

Roosevelt brought in some money himself as a youngster. He had a shoeshine box, and he also ran errands for prostitutes, including steering customers to them. "I spent a lot of time in the 50s hanging around honky-tonks."

Roosevelt said that by the time he was twelve or thirteen he'd seen five people murdered.

His father's cousin was a trapper, and Roosevelt would help him trap mink and tan the hides. They'd also go out at night and dig up turtles.

From around the age of ten or eleven, he also did chores for the local mortician. "He taught me about, discipline, honesty, integrity, respect," Roosevelt said. The mortician, who'd been a friend of Roosevelt's father, wanted the young man to come into business with him and even offered to put him through college. But by the time he was eighteen, Lewis was tired of death. "The mortician was a good man, but there is no substitute for your own father," Roosevelt said. Lewis's mother never talked about how his father died, so Lewis didn't know until he was a teenager and heard the story from some of the older men.

One morning in 1950, his father went to the store to get something for breakfast. As he was leaving, a white man came out with his own bags and said, "Boy, I want you to load these groceries into my car."

"My dad refused," Lewis said, "and he walked away. The man backed his vehicle into my father and killed him."

Lewis grew up feeling sheltered from racism. "I dealt with racism," he said, "but I was surrounded by all these black men and women in this black community, so I shook it off." That changed as he got older and began looking to his future.

In ninth grade, he got into trouble when the school superintendent came to his school and said things about the black teachers that offended Lewis. Lewis wrote to the superintendent about the comments, which caused problems for the school. To mollify the superintendent, the principal found a spot for Lewis at a nearby trade school.

Lewis learned how to repair radios and televisions and earned his radio and TV repair certificate.

He couldn't find a job, so he decided to leave town. A friend suggested joining the Army. "So January 10, 1967, I raised my right hand." After training, he went off to Germany and then to fight in Vietnam. He got out of the Army at Ft. Lewis, in Tacoma, Washington, his first connection to the Northwest. Before the war, Lewis said, "I was a solid, stable guy. I came back a train wreck. I didn't know what was wrong. I couldn't sleep. I was afraid of the dark. I wanted to be armed all the time." He'd gotten married his last year in the Army and that wasn't working out. He had problems, and she had problems too. After five years, "finally she just packed up and left," with their son, he said. Lewis worked for Washington State ferries for several years, but finally he ended up in a Veteran's Administration psych ward in 1974 and 1975 with post traumatic stress disorder. After he was released, he was jobless and homeless, battling nightmares, and reliving experiences from Vietnam.

He went back to Louisiana in 1978 worn down by PTSD and alcoholism. He entered a new long-term experimental program for alcoholics at the Veteran's Hospital in Shreveport, Louisiana. He stayed in this program for two years. While there, his mother died. Afterwards he came back to Seattle.

He started over, washing windows. He went into the painting business, then started a janitorial business. He began buying houses to sell, and he met his future wife. He climbed out of the bottle completely and has been off alcohol for more than thirty-six years.

"Working for myself helped," he said. "I was able to take care of myself, get a foundation under myself, and get back in the church. Life is so good."

As he continues to move forward, his art work keeps Lewis rooted. He didn't think of what he did as art early on. Making things just gave him pleasure. "When I was a child, art was essential to my life and remains so today."

"In Natchitoches, I used to go down to the garbage dump and pick up all sorts of things," Lewis said. He'd use what he found to make anything his mind came up with. "I used to call myself an inventor. I didn't know the word art."

His inventions first morphed into art, after he noticed the art that white people had on their walls and in their yards. He was always looking for a way to bring in a little money, so he made his own objects. What he made was dictated by what the white women would buy.

"My first piece was a flower basket made from clothes hangers that I got from a garbage dump," Lewis said. "Often I saw a concrete sculpture of little Black Sambo on the steps of wealthy home owners. I used the red mud from the side of a hill and shaped it into a sculptured piece. Wire bird cages were to follow."

The first praise he remembers getting for his work was from a woman who bought a yellow bird cage from him for $5. Lewis said he felt a real sense of accomplishment walking through the segregated neighborhood and seeing his work hanging from the porch.

But, he said, "I never understood myself to be an artist until many years later."

There is no question about that these days. Roosevelt Lewis is an artist. He's won praise and awards for his artistry, and his work has been shown in galleries throughout the Northwest. But it is clear where his heart is by the label he applies to his work, Cane River Fine Arts.

Taught by Life

I don't think I should strive to create art outside of the world in which I have evolved. The environment I grew up in dictates that I am honest about the lives of the people I paint about. My hope is that my observations about black people living in a specific region are accepted universally.

Many of my works move between abstraction and metaphor, lines and planes. On the other hand, the characters in my paintings show meaning and depth of purpose, whether it is a single person or a group scene. I've tried to empower the situation one sees in my paintings, because poverty and wealth—struggling black poor and working middle class—lived side by side in the black neighborhood at that time.

I believe my work is a reflection of the possibilities of moving one generation beyond the other. Artistically, I will continue to believe my paintings are a part of the American experience.

Roosevelt Lewis

Jackson Square

In the 1950s, Jackson Square in Natchitoches (NAK a dish), Louisiana, was a thriving black paradise, bordered by railroad tracks to the east, swamps to the north, and lying along Cane River and a lake. Cotton was the crop that fueled the economy during that time. Jackson Square supplied the labor for the nearby rich, lush farmlands. However, paper mills and plywood manufacturing began to open up throughout the Parish. Chicken processing plants soon followed.

There were no sociological or ideological struggles in Natchitoches, unlike the Civil Rights unrest that was escalating across the South during that time, because African Americans had a deeper level of fear of losing what progress they had made with the white power structure that controlled the economy. The community was sedate, while the rest of the South was pressing for freedom. The streets in the neighborhoods were full of black life and suppressed pain. French Colonial architecture and unkept drainage ditches met well-kept sidewalks that led to homes of well-to-do, aristocratic whites.

The seeds of my life were nurtured by these indelible memories of Southern segregation and not knowing my place or what was right or wrong socially. My paintings and sculptures depict the proud people of the Cane River region who tried to teach me to live beyond my immediate experiences. Some of those lessons were abstract, others were physical.

Artries

My mama, Artries, got pregnant by one of her brothers when she was fourteen years old. When her mother and father found out, they considered it a dishonor for the family in their small farming community of Three Leaf Bayou in Powhaton, Louisiana, about twenty miles outside of Natchitoches. Mama said, after she had the baby, "It was hard living at home." A few years later, she was sent to live on her own with her child and a few raggedy clothes. It was about 1935 when she arrived in Natchitoches with her son, Spike, in tow. She had lost her hearing a few years earlier and with no formal training in the use of sign language, she had to learn to read lips with the circle of friends she made in the Natchitoches colored community of Jackson Circle.

She was befriended by a woman named Mama June who lived in an old, unpainted, single-story house with a sagging tin roof. Curtains made from empty cotton flower bags hung at the windows. The backdrop was a cemetery. The winter was cold and unforgiving the day they came to town, and she thanked God for Mama June. There wasn't enough room for her and her son at Mama June's, but Mama didn't know when they could move into their own house.

She had to leave little Spike home while doing domestic work in nearby white communities. At work they thought she was dumb because she could not hear what they told her to do. Mama said it was hard working for white folks at first, but then they saw her reading a book from their library shelf. After that, they would write the housework instructions for her.

Before Mama lost her hearing, she was the best student in her class. White people wouldn't let colored people study past seventh grade in those days, but that was equivalent to a high school diploma back then.

The white man Mama worked for made her go to bed with him one day. Then he wanted to have sex with her all of the time, so she quit her job and struggled to feed herself and her son. Work in nearby fields was scarce when they got to town, since cotton harvesting had been completed. Mama said the men who worked on the railroad came to town once a week, and she made them happy, and they gave her money. That's how she and Spike survived until things got better. With what little money she had going to buy food, Mama had to rely on the gratitude of others for clothes and shoes.

Mama said she met my father on a visit back home to Three Leaf Bayou. Mama had medium brown skin and was short in stature. Her long, wavy hair derived from her Choctaw Indian ancestry. She said Daddy was seduced by her good looks right away. He had come across Red River on the old wooden ferry boat from St. John's, Louisiana, his home. He was twenty years her senior, and they had a one-year courtship that led to

Artries

Acrylic on canvas
48" x 24½"
2003

marriage. She said she did not love him, but needed a secure home for her son to grow up in. Soon they moved into a rundown house near Mama June's place. Mama was happy to have her own home because my sister was already on the way. A year after my sister, I was born. Mama cried a lot about how Daddy treated little Spike. He was physically abusive to him all the time and showed favoritism toward me and my sister. The mistreatment of my brother would affect our lives as a family well into the future.

Daddy worked for the railroad and left home for long periods of time. He always brought gifts home for me and my sister. Spike got nothing but more bad treatment. Mama said Spike wanted to know who his father was as he got older, but she just couldn't bring herself to tell him. She suffered carrying that secret around. It was like being chained to a tree. During those early years, she cried a lot about that first pregnancy. Gossip had begun to spread about who Spike's father was, which forced her to isolate herself from her extended family.

Mama allowed another man to come into her life during Daddy's long journeys away. Skip Lee brought gifts and gave Mama money when Daddy was gone and after he died, too. His visits were short, but continued for years. I was impressed by his style of clothes. He was a tall, well-dressed, mulatto man; his shoes were shined, and his shirt was starched and hot pressed. He was soft spoken. Sometimes when he came, Mama would fry chicken and make biscuits for him to take on his journey back home. I overheard Mama saying he had moved to Shreveport and had a wife and children. They dated until his wife demanded that he stop.

Mama said I was seven years old when Daddy left us to go to heaven. Skip came to his funeral. He stayed around that night. Mama told me and my sister to go to bed early. My sister, Ulah, always obeyed. I lay in bed awake. Soon the bed springs began to squeak real slowly. Then the squeak got faster and faster. I plugged my ears with my fingers, but the sound from bed springs coming from my mother's room got louder, and then just when I thought it wouldn't stop, the squeaking got slower and slower and then stopped. For a few minutes, it was quiet in the house. It wasn't long before I heard the rusty hinges on the front door open and close. The unpainted, broken down, creaky steps could be heard through the door. I knew Skip had left the house, and I was satisfied and went to sleep.

The next day Mama was in the kitchen making homemade biscuits. She had already sliced smoked bacon and was laying it neatly in a big, black, iron skillet. The flames from the gas stove burner radiated around the skillet bottom. Soon the aroma of that smoked bacon filled the three-room house.

Every time I heard the springs creaking at night in Mama's bedroom, the next day she had more money to spend on food and extra items for the house. She would send me to buy the groceries and pay monthly bills before they were due. My sister and I would get an extra treat.

After Daddy died, Mama said she needed liquor to help her sleep. She would send me to the store to buy it with a note in a brown paper bag. The note read, "Mr. Ned, please give my son half a pint of Early Times. The money is in the bag. Thanks. Artries."

Eventually, after spending my childhood buying liquor for Mama, I became brave enough to ask for a drink from her bottle. I was about twelve years old when she poured the liquor bottle cap full of whiskey and gave it to me. A year after my first drink it took larger amounts to satisfy me. Two years passed, and I was drinking even larger quantities. One day, Mama decided to buy me my own bottle of alcohol. At that point, I found in alcohol what I could not find without it, a way to endure the constant anxiety of living in my mother's environment.

With all of Mama's efforts, we struggled to make ends meet. We had no hot running water in our home nor an indoor bathroom. An old, outdoor wood-frame toilet stood just feet from the kitchen door. The smell and embarrassment of having to use it took its toll.

One day when I was intoxicated, I poured lighter fluid over one of my mother's boyfriend's leather shoes. Lighting it gave me pleasure; anger followed because he did not burn to death. Fear that my mother was going to be killed was a constant with this boyfriend. They both fought often, pulling out knives and threatening to kill each other. Money was always the central theme in their arguments. Alcohol was a close second.

Drinking alcohol helped me escape my dysfunctional home. My personality evolved. An intelligent, well-read kid, I was subservient to whites in order to earn money. I kept secrets for educated blacks. I was well-mannered to my godfather and church members, yet I was a depressed youth trying to figure out what the next day would be like in my mother's home. Would she get drunk? Or would she be the kind and gentle mother I knew she could be without the influence of the cunning drug, alcohol.

As Mama became addicted to alcohol, she became less able to see the damage she was doing to her children. From Monday to Wednesday we had a short break from Mama's drunkenness and hangovers, but Thursday it started all over again. Cleaning up her vomit and feces from the floor during her alcoholic blackouts took a toll on our young lives. By this time, my sister was fourteen, and my mother pestered her about earning her keep by having sex with a thirty-year-old Creole man who had asked to marry her. He lived across the street.

Mama was desperate about not wanting to take one step backwards toward the poverty she had begun to overcome. Everything was on the table when it came to getting enough money, even hustling her daughter. Ulah was an ebony-eyed, mulatto woman with good looks that caught the eyes of many older men in the neighborhood. She felt Mama shouldn't have been trying to give her away to an older man because she was still a child. Sometimes my sister would lie across the bed and bury her head in a pillow and cry. When Ulah turned fifteen, she was tired of Mama screaming at her to have sex with older men. Mama did not want her to pick her own boyfriends, but my sister found a man and told him if he brought liquor and food, Mama would allow him to come and go as he pleased.

My sister's dysfunctional childhood forced her to grow up too soon and left her unprepared for life. It followed her into her marriage and contaminated her relationship with her children. Mama was angry with Ulah's choice of husband and reminded her of it often. Mama didn't like him because she and his mother were dating the same man.

Ulah began to drink alcohol to numb her feelings. Her relationship with Mama was never good again. She and her husband eventually divorced, and she never recovered mentally or emotionally. In the end, it destroyed all of her sense of self-worth. She died a debilitated alcoholic at the age of sixty-one.

My sister had three children. Her oldest son died in his late thirties. Her second son got married, finished college, and achieved great success in life, though his relationship with his mother had diminished by the time of her death. Her daughter went unprepared into a marriage where she has found more challenges than joys.

Mama always did special things for Spike. She would give him her last dime. She repeatedly borrowed money from her bank to give to him, even though she was receiving Supplemental Security Income and it would take her years to pay it back. Spike made Mama feel guilty about the secret of his parentage. She suppressed her feelings to protect his pain throughout her life.

As my mother's health declined, she could not drink as much alcohol. Her poor eating habits and clogged arteries and arthritis slowed her down. Mama had a massive stroke but couldn't be treated at the local hospital because she did not have medical insurance. Two months earlier, Spike had convinced her to cancel her Medicaid Health Insurance to save four dollars. She died in a nursing home for indigent people two months later. Spike cashed her life insurance policy and refused to bury her. She was finally buried in an unmarked grave near her ancestors on Three Leaf Bayou.

The Field

Black sun, burned hands
pick the cotton bolls
stalks await a tiller's fold.

Tired driven stooped backs
spirits lift in song
at dawn till no more sun.

Dirty sweat-soaked faces
board cattle bed trucks
a solemn journey home.

Tin-roof-top shacks
greet their worn frames
winter fills the rooms.

A gas heater whispers
splayed flames of pleasure
dreary drawn bodies massed.

Hog-fat grease sizzles
hot water bread frying
slaughter house scraps refined.

Roaches nibble on crumbs
damp with sugar water drops
their babies swarm sugar nipple rags.

Stomach fed with rinds
spirit lifted with love drops
in body heat they sleep.

Chained beyond bondage and freedom.

Cush

My uncle Cush, my mother's youngest brother, was born in 1924 and grew up on a farm that my grandfather purchased on Three Leaf Bayou, a small village in Powhatan, Louisiana, where generations of our family had lived. Cush was the youngest of eight children. On the family farm, food was plentiful; Granddaddy raised vegetables, hogs, and chickens, which he shared with other neighbors who were less fortunate.

Cush loved and admired his father and mother. They were the glue that held his life together. Home was a safe and peaceful place for him to be. But one day my grandfather got sick, and soon after died. My grandmother was left to run their family farm. All of her children pitched in to help her.

Cush

In the 1920s blacks lived under constant fear of losing their land or life to a system of segregation and oppression. One day a knock on the door changed their lives forever. A tax assessor had come to serve notice to vacate their premises for an unproven tax debt. Cush's uneducated mother was forced to sign her name with an "X" on a document she could neither read nor question.

The children suffered after losing their father. It was equally painful to see their mother crying at the loss of their home. Grief took a toll on her life. A few years later, in a small, broken-down house, she succumbed to death, surrounded by her children. The children moved away to large and small cities. Cush, the youngest, became enraged at the white world because he felt it had killed his mother. He had grown tall, with good looks that filled women with desire for his muscular body. But he resented the racial boundaries placed on his life, and as he matured, he was known to turn his anger on others. In nearby Natchitoches, he fought and broke more than a few limbs. Local nightclub patrons and business owners alike feared him.

The rest of Cush's family suffered the indignity of racism without resorting to violence, choosing education instead. The 1940s came, and World War II was raging in France. Cush joined the fight thinking he would earn respect back home. The war for him and other black soldiers proved to be a bitter experience. The racism in the army increased his anger until it pushed him over the edge and sent him on a killing spree against soldiers from the all-white army unit. He landed in stockade. While he was there, to force him to confess, they pulled out his toenails with pliers. Though he was tortured, he would not admit to killing the white soldiers.

He was brought back to the United States to stand trial and heal from the torture in a prison hospital. While there, he kidnapped a male and a female staff member. He later freed them and escaped to a midwestern town.

He found a job on a ranch working for a widowed white woman with whom he developed a relationship. Ten years passed, and he finally made a mistake. He sent a letter to his favorite sister, Artries, using his real return address. A few months later, the FBI agents who'd been trailing him captured him outside the store where he bought his monthly carton of cigarettes. He was brought back to stand trial, only to find that witnesses to the crime could not be found and evidence regarding his case had been lost.

After a few years in prison, Cush was released and moved to Houston, Texas, where he started a family. But he developed a severe drinking problem that contributed to his death from lobar pneumonia at age sixty-six. His violence against his wife was unspeakable. After years of beatings and abuse, she left in the middle of the night with their children. In researching this story, I learned that they continue to suffer post traumatic stress disorder, depression, and anxiety.

Cush was part of a generation in 1940s America who obeyed whites, and he hid his rage as long as he could.

When things went wrong in the army, killing whites became his answer. Responding to his oppressive environment, he mistakenly, sadly, brutalized and killed innocent people.

Racism was the poison that drove Cush's behavior. His physical wounds may have healed but his psychic and emotional wounds never did. America just poured salt on those wounds. This was the experience of most African Americans growing up in the South and elsewhere in this country, during that time and even now.

Natchitoches

The French and Spanish architecture overlooking Cane River is a part of a historic journey in the evolution of the oldest city in the Louisiana Purchase. The quiet calm of Cane River runs deep with stories of war and surrender. Along her shores, cotton and indigo crops once grew, while Indian tepees stood among a tribal nation of warriors and hunters who have come and gone. Downtown Natchitoches (NAK-a-dish) overlooks this silent body of water with a visible charm that hides the bitter memories in her past.

A red brick street reflects the African slave artisans who handcrafted Front Street and harvested the labor-intensive crops that helped fuel the economy. Wealthy and poverty-stricken Negroes could be found window shopping together on most any day.

In the 1950s on Horn Street in downtown Natchitoches, Negroes congregated outside Antee's Barbershop and the nearby bar on Saturdays after a hard week's work.

A block away, families lined up outside the segregated Cane Movie Theatre where they escaped for a while. Across the street from the theater was a Trailways bus station fitted with signs with arrows that pointed the way to whites-only sections of the building.

One block south of the bus station was the courthouse filled with segregated water fountains and restrooms. Colored janitors kept the place spotless. The psychological boundaries could not be disputed and were evident in the laws that governed differences in social and economic status. South of the courthouse at Second Street was Zestos hamburger drive-in where Negroes waited their turn after whites were served and had left.

At sunrise on Monday mornings throughout the colored community, the population of white women increased dramatically. They were in the neighborhood to chauffeur their maids back to their private residences to work. Being chauffeured to work was the one time a domestic worker could feel a sense of social acceptance by white people, although employees were relegated to the back seat. The pay for domestic work was small, but important in the life of female workers at that time. The well manicured lawns and upscale living always reminded the domestic laborers where their place was in society.

Organizations, such as the Daughters of the Confederacy, the John Birch Society, and the Ku Klux Klan maintained a subtle chokehold on the very lives of those who had cooked, cleaned, and cared for their old, sick, young, and physically capable family members.

The color line that stretched from one end of Cane River to the other was not a barrier at all when it came to sexual pleasures. It was a paradox taking place among whites and coloreds in Natchitoches, especially between colored women and the white men who were ejaculating into their wombs. Children from these oppressed relationships were given separate identities that designated them mulatto.

From slave times to the 1950s, mulattos were given preferences by their masters and later by local employers. It caused passive resistance from their dark-skinned counterparts. The contradiction in Natchitoches continued; integration brought hope, but left despair. Today, blacks earn better wages, but illiteracy is running rampant. Neighborhoods excite more fear than pleasure.

White and colored descendants have become fused together, and perhaps will be for another five hundred years of unpredictable chronic inequality and predetermined failure in historic Natchitoches.

Cane River runs quiet and calm through the passage of time.

Front Street, Natchitoches

Photograph by Jarred Hamilton, 2014

Stories and Art

Torn Roots

*T*orn Roots is a monument to a father who went shopping one Sunday morning for food to cook breakfast for his son and never returned. The sculpture is carved wood of a dark maple and of a walnut tree whose grain quality, tone, and workability were perfect.

I wanted to do a large-scale sculpture as a tribute to my father. The absence of my father left a blank space that could only be filled by creating art that reflected what I remembered of his strength, courage, and resolve. Most of my memories of him had been erased by time so I decided to return to Louisiana to research the mystery of how he died.

His old friends shared with me a graphic account of his final minutes of life. They said Daddy loved cooking breakfast for me and my sister on Sunday mornings. And every Sunday, he walked the short distance to Berry's Market down the nearby railroad tracks to purchase food to cook. On April 16, 1950, at 8:00 A.M. on Sunday morning, as he left the store clutching his groceries, a white man who had driven up demanded that my father drop his groceries and attend to the needs of his family.

My father refused and started back home. He paused briefly to speak to his friends, who were sitting nearby. A few seconds later the driver drove into him and crushed his body against the store wall. The groceries scattered from his arms. He was pronounced dead at the scene. A week later, he was buried.

I thought a lasting work of art would resolve my quest and end my physical search. Memories can take on many shapes and forms artistically. In my attempt to explore my father's last goodbye to me, I settled on the image of an arm torn from his body, chained at the wrist, with hands reaching for life. I attached his portrait, based on the only photograph I have of him, to the upper portion of the sculpture.

Life is like an old-growth tree; left to grow undisturbed, it will thrive of its own accord. It will wind its way toward the stars and look out over the valleys and rivers while waiting on a chance to be cared for and made beautiful, to grow in other ways, loved and admired as a family heirloom or antique that may end up traveling to some foreign land, returning at some point to live out life, old but in good hands.

As the stories about my father progressed, his Choctaw Indian ancestry was revealed. Now filled with excitement, I knew the roots were not torn, but connected to a rich cultural past of history and grandeur.

This sculpture is inescapably influenced by place and time, whether it is the war I fought in, or poverty I lived in, or the pain of the loss of a father. I invite you into this visual revelation of the hope and dreams of a son whose art embodies the American experience of love, joy, struggle, and forgiveness.

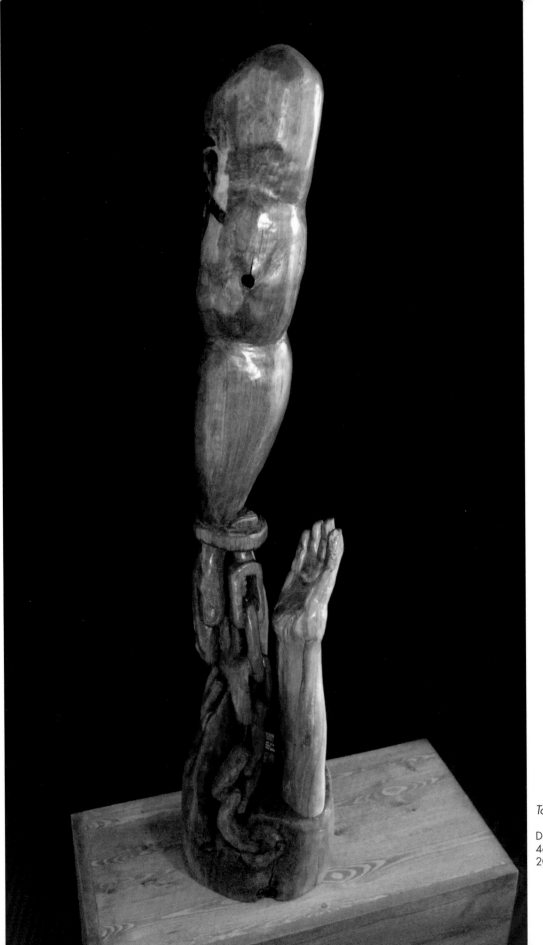

Torn Roots

Dark maple and walnut
46¾" x 10" x 10"
2008

Do No More Violence To Women

In 1950s in Louisiana, there was no broad public awareness of violence against African American women. Local newspapers made few announcements regarding abuse of these women. That these women were unable to assert their rights in the voting booths or help shape domestic policy in state elections did not concern the lawmakers, who could have made a difference by protecting battered women.

Most of these women stayed in abusive marriages for economic reasons and for the sake of their children. Fear of the abusive husband and the difficulty of starting a new life were other reasons. Children living in homes devastated by domestic violence were left to deal with this emotional roller coaster by themselves. It did not matter whether they became educated or gained access to good opportunities.

The struggle for success in life was a perilous path for many of the abused. Drugs, anger, and bitterness derailed some of the children permanently. It was not unusual to find that a good portion of the prison population were young, angry black men and women who had suffered in households where violence occurred. Furthermore, the damage caused by violent abuse is transferred through generations from a system of learned behavior and must be dealt with through psychiatric intervention.

Young men and women who endured the physical and emotional carnage inflicted on them developed violent responses to the world they live in and are more likely to fail in marriage and parenting.

Some of the women who survived years of abusive marriages where the criminal justice system did not protect them took the law into their own hands. Most often, this action meant death to the abuser and an end to the years of senseless pain for helpless wives and children. At this juncture, the legal system that would not protect these women would work to put them in prison.

Women who face a terminal point in their lives by committing an act of violence against an abusive husband and going to prison demonstrate how violence against women destroys homes, communities, and children's futures.

The amount of money spent to deal with the problems caused by domestic abuse and violent homes suggests that we should pay more attention to early intervention and provide more support for victims of domestic abuse.

In communities that direct their efforts toward relieving the plight of women and children in violent homes, everyone benefits.

Do No More Violence to Women

Walnut
19½" x 20" x 7"
2000

Generations of Women

In this painting, a mother embraces her daughters after church. She is a widow who has tried to raise them to be responsible young women. Bonding at an early age has helped shape their alliances with each other. But loving and giving children the right values does not guarantee that they will avoid serious problems as they go through life. The pitfalls in life are many and can be a prevailing factor as a child evolves into adulthood.

In the 1950s, in Natchitoches, Louisiana, on Jackson Square, a woman with three daughters faced unforeseen challenges. Economic disparity was one of the central reasons that African American women had to accept low-paying jobs with no other options to care for their families. Difficult as the conditions were, many young adults took the path to success by attending college. Others were not as fortunate. Planned Parenthood was not available to young women who became pregnant. The consequences meant that their children would be raised in predetermined circumstances, such as failing schools, unavailable health care, or no access to libraries, guaranteeing fewer job opportunities, and their families would suffer the same fate, too. Women who are forced to marry too young do not mature in the right way. They remain undeveloped socially far into their adult years.

The church was very supportive to many mothers during this time. Believing their faith was a cure against racism and the oppressed conditions of that time was the hope they needed for a better life.

The oldest of the three daughters in the painting went through a ten-year cycle of drug addiction and prostitution. The daughter is recovering and trying to regain her place in society. The mother raised her daughter's child who has suffered through the long absence of her mother. The mother and daughter are healing, but the child is trying to find a way to connect to her mother again. Good childhood memories are important, and when they are lost they cannot be easily recaptured. The middle daughter is trying to support her oldest sister, but domestic violence by an ex-husband resulted in her being committed to a mental institution for years, until she was released into the care of her mother. The courts gave custody of her children to their father who was never seen again.

In church, the youngest daughter gave testimony that her father had sexually abused her at an early age. The psychological trauma of rape has continued to disrupt her life. The mother struggles with overwhelming guilt because she blindfolded herself to her husband's actions against her daughter.

Raising three daughters under any circumstances is a challenge for a widowed mother. Redeeming her life is the one goal she seeks in order to help turn her daughters' lives around.

Generations of Women

Acrylic on illustration board
29½" x 32½"
2001

Washing Clothes

On Saturday mornings as the hot southern sun rose up over the tall pecan trees in Powhatan, Louisiana, near Red River, African American mothers gathered their clothes to wash by hand. In the 1950s in small towns and country roads, washing machines did not exist for the majority of women. They lived in long, narrow, three-room houses, with no hot or cold running water. The houses were clustered together and separated by racial patterns that were normal at that time. A metal tub placed at the end of a back porch was filled with water from a neighborhood water faucet. Dirty clothes were pushed down into the tub, where they soaked before being washed on a rub board made from wood and tin.

They washed the clothes with a bar of lye soap. A five-cent piece of lye soap purchased from a lye maker who peddled his product throughout the Parish would last them for weeks. They hung their clothes from a wire line stretched between wood poles set a distance apart. While women washed, their children played nearby. They thumb-shot marbles in a round ring drawn in the dirt, or threw horse shoes at metal stakes that had been hammered into the ground. It was a way for children to develop the same bonds that their parents had been able to hang on to. Money was not plentiful but many of these mothers had learned to band together to ease the constant struggles in their lives.

Washing clothes during the winter months brought families close together. The metal tub was moved inside the house to the kitchen. Since there was no water in the house, the women carried buckets of water from the outdoor faucet, heated it on the gas cook stove, and poured it into the wash tub. In the winter, indoor clothes lines were stretched over the gas heater used to warm the room. Clothespins attached garments to the line.

In the early morning, white women could be seen unloading large bundles of clothes onto front porches in the community because African American women washed clothes for profit along with their regular wash. Their clothes were starched, hot ironed, and picked up within days. Loyalty between these black and white women has existed for centuries in spite of inequality among the races.

Women who washed together attended the same church services where they developed lasting spiritual bonds for themselves, their children, and generations that followed.

Washing Clothes

Acrylic on paper
20½" x 18½"
2000

Godfather's Guiding Hands

Godfathers in Central Louisiana found their way into the lives of young African American men in many ways. Some of the ways were through churches, community centers, and athletics, keeping young men occupied with constructive activities that provided positive growth as they matured. The bountiful fishing and hunting throughout the community made bonding between godfathers and young men easy. Fatherless boys could be easily identified in small towns where every neighbor was a friend.

Godfather's Guiding Hands represents the patience men had in teaching life skills. This meant the difference between success and failure in a child's life. These men had unblemished integrity and strong spiritual values, which set them apart from other men unwilling to take on building young lives. Many of these men were members of an African American Masonic Lodge, a secret order that was well respected in the community. They were also low-skilled workers who had endured fleeting opportunities.

My godfather was a large man of considerable strength who ate round steaks and drank large glasses of ice tea. He was a chef and self-taught carpenter who shared his talents for building houses and growing gardens with me. His home was on a half acre of land with a large chicken house. Dozens of chickens populated the property, too. It was a place for lifelong learning that followed me into adulthood.

Godfathers were traditional in the African American church. A godfather's role in the life of a newborn child started with a baptism and prayer of commitment to the child's growing life. Some of this ceremony can be traced to the African continent where communal living and tribal unity were essential to survival.

Currently, mentoring programs have replaced the role that godfathers fulfilled a half century ago. Those charged with helping young men find meaning in their lives face problems far more complex today. Because of an epidemic of drugs, violence, and deterioration of the family structure, communities throughout our great country are trying to find a formula to stem the tide of incarceration, recidivism, and death among young African American men. Tomorrow's communities will be faced with developing new generations of godfathers who are more focused on education and who use statistically proven ideas that reflect the multi-cultural society we have become. Giving children love and attention should be a universal goal and should remain the hallmark of the role of godfathers in children's success in life.

Godfather's Guiding Hands

Acrylic on illustration board
42¼" x 32¼"
2008

Freddie's Place

Freddie wanted to be a great double bass musician, but he became a restaurant owner who sold barbeque ribs instead. From Friday to Sunday on Jackson Square in Natchitoches you could smell the aroma of meat cooking on an outdoor barbeque pit from three blocks away. Inside the restaurant, barbeque ribs were sold to a hungry clientele from across a countertop.

A doorway led to the liquor bar and dance floor. Some customers crowded onto the dance floor while others sat at small wooden booths. The loud juke box played blues and jazz. Alcoholics lined a wood-framed bar where Old Taylor whiskey and Jacks beer quenched their thirst.

Most weekend nights, a Southern Pacific freight train could be heard rumbling along the tracks behind the restaurant. For a few minutes, it would drown out the music and conversations throughout the restaurant. No one paused for the interruption.

Freddie's Place was where marriages were broken, while widows and divorcees could be seen leaving with some young, smooth-talking man looking for a meal and a place to lay his head.

Old gamblers stopped by late at night after winning a few dollars looking for young, big-busted, single women to spend their money with. Middle-class members of the community stopped by, too. They were the teachers and preachers picking up their barbeque orders to go. Most of them were secret alcoholics who had their half pints of liquor placed in the bottom of a bag and covered over by an order of barbeque.

After church on Sunday, members of the Usher Board would stop by Freddie's to eat. Some of them would stay until dark. Some of them would find themselves on the dance floor moving and swaying to the music.

The armistice that ended the Korean War in 1953 brought thousands of African American soldiers to nearby Fort Polk, Louisiana. They pitched their large green tents near the Natchitoches city limits. This became their living quarters for several years. Many of these soldiers spent weekends at Freddie's Place socializing with local residents. Prostitutes were there looking for a way to feed their young babies and pay their bills. After a couple of years, the army troops moved on, leaving behind fatherless sons and daughters to find their way through life without them.

After the troop withdrawal, some people drifted out of town, seeking better jobs and higher pay in larger cities. Older prostitutes went back to doing domestic work, and the younger women of that profession found whatever means they had to provide for themselves. Some of these women found good husbands, and had children who went on to college and became outstanding citizens.

But the party never stopped at Freddie's.

Freddie's Place

Acrylic on illustration board
42½" x 22½"
2000

Father and Baby

Father and Baby portrays an African American father who has just returned home from a hard day's work. His lunch container is on the floor next to him. He cuddles the baby close to his body. In the 1950s in Central Louisiana, it was a rare sight to witness a black father nurturing his child in such a personal way because the turn of the century had not been kind to black men.

This painting represents fathers who were born in the 1900s with no tangible way to guarantee success for their child's future, but who remained in their lives despite the difficulties of the time. *Father and Baby* shows that love for one's child does not cost money and can be replicated from one father's heart to another. The importance of a man's role in a child's life does not exclude the influence women have on a child. They are important, too, as teachers, nurses, daycare providers, social workers, and just plain good mothers. Both parents are important to the full development of a child. Fathers and mothers together is what we should strive for. This painting shows one half of the goal of being a better parent to our children.

Hard, intensive labor, low pay, and long hours took a toll on a man's ability to be a good father, yet the presence of a father encouraged other members of the community to support men. For example, in an unwritten code of conduct, other men in the community taught young black men how to survive in that particular time in their history. Yet children often became casualties resulting from limitations placed on fathers who could not provide the right kind of resources for them. At the same time, this region produced a supply of well-educated black men. They served as military officers, infantry soldiers, college professors, educators, and community builders, not only in the Cane River area but throughout the country.

This painting is about the importance of men in the lives of their children. The children of loving parents receive the best early childhood development. Fathers who participate in their children's lives are pivotal as those children grow and become active members of a community. Having a good father helps anchor children in the black community as well as the nation as a whole. Good intergenerational fatherhood strengthens our society against the epidemic of violence and drugs. Life becomes reciprocal for each successive generation in our effort to create a better world.

Father and Baby

Acrylic on illustration board
32" x 42"
2006

The Barber Shop

In the African American community on Jackson Square in Natchitoches, one barber shop stood out from all the others. For most of the customers who walked through the door, it was more than just a place to get a haircut. Inside there were two barber chairs, a shoeshine stand, a toilet, and a small room where liquor was stored. The two well-respected barbers could be found solving family problems or debating about sports, women, and race relations in the community.

Men gathered around an old beat-up radio on Friday nights to listen to the boxing matches. The shoeshine boy was busy boiling hot link sausages in the kitchen on an electric stove. He was the barber shop waiter who ran errands and made phone calls to cheating wives who met secretly in dubious places. What appeared to be a shoeshine stand operation in the corner of a barber shop was actually a small enterprise that benefitted cheating husbands and filled the shoeshiner's pockets with tips and bribes.

As the shoeshine boy grew into manhood, the legs, breasts, and hips of these tempting, cheating women aroused his sexual interest, too. His secretive phone calls on behalf of other men to married ladies began to serve his self-interest. Soon these older women were spending their money on him.

The barber shop was a place where gamblers gathered for a drink of whiskey and a shoeshine and haircut before going next door to the gambling shack. The shoeshine boy would work the shack until late in the night delivering food and liquor to the gamblers.

The barber shop held informal meetings about problems in the neighborhood, much like African traditions where elders and leaders of their respective villages came together to choose what was best for their people. However, there was broad dissent among people in the community regarding who was decent enough to be called their leader.

Connected to the back of the barber shop was a beauty salon. On Saturday afternoons, women would traverse a narrow walkway that led to an entrance to the salon. African American women placed a great deal of emphasis on how they looked, after years of passive resistance to unequal social treatment that left many women seeking equality through their appearance.

The barber shop, though corrupt in its drinking, gambling, and adultery, was a place where financially secure men and women came together with the struggling poor and the hustlers and gamblers in a powerless pursuit of assimilation into a society not ready to receive them with open arms.

The Barber Shop

Acrylic on illustration board
43" x 32"
1999

A Lesson Before Crying

I was filled with emotions and anticipation as the landing gear locked in place for the final approach to Oakland air terminal in California. I thought about the love of my life as the plane descended over the Pacific Ocean waves. Eighteen hundred miles separated me from her and my home in Natchitoches.

Twenty-six months earlier in January, 1967 in Shreveport, I had raised my right hand and sworn to defend the constitution of the United States at a U.S. Army induction station. All of the fourteen southern states were still legally segregated. Racism was rampant even though black and white soldiers were fighting together in Vietnam.

Now it was March 21, 1969, and I was returning home from Vietnam to a country in turmoil. The day I arrived back in the States, blacks were rioting in major American cities, and civil disobedience had brought unrest everywhere in the country.

Dr. Martin Luther King's death had occurred April 4, 1968, three weeks after I arrived in Vietnam. It was a sad day for black soldiers. The killing of a black leader weighed heavily on our minds, and it left me struggling to cope with my feelings. Black soldiers in Vietnam were implicated in bombings after his assassination. Platoon leaders maintained control over black troops by threatening to shoot them for treason. Some men involved in the bombings were imprisoned in Long Binh Jail in 1968 because they refused to continue to take part in combat patrols. Dr. King's death created a morale problem in the jails, causing inmates to riot at Long Binh Jail. They beat white inmates and attacked guards. Most of these men were dishonorably discharged and faced a lifetime of rejection in employment from the stigma associated with failed military service.

But the war raged on, and a few weeks after the prison riots, I was on a mission deep into an enemy stronghold. The Chinook helicopter I was riding in near Loc Ninh was hit by enemy bullets that tore though one engine. We went down hard into a rubber tree plantation. We were quickly rescued and flown to Bien Hoa hospital. Two of our troops died, and I suffered a concussion. A few weeks later I returned to my company. I felt blessed to be alive and to have survived without serious injury.

During my year in Vietnam, I went on hundreds of aerial and ground combat missions. On one of the missions, we made contact with the enemy and were pinned down in a rubber tree plantation. One of my buddies told me to switch positions with him. After he took my position, he was hit in the head by a bullet and died instantly. The move had saved my life, and I have never forgotten him.

Returning to our base after a mission gave me a chance to refocus my mind for a short time. I looked forward to clean clothes, a hot meal, and a chance to read letters from home. One of the worst things that could happen to a soldier was a Dear John letter. These letters from wives seeking a divorce or girlfriends ending their relationships were devastating. Some men clung desperately to their relationships, others committed suicide. Some remained distraught for the rest of their tour duty.

If I survived the war, I looked forward to marriage and children. Letters from my girlfriend had stopped coming two months prior to my departure from Vietnam but I would not allow myself to believe we did not have a bright future together. Even reading her old letters made me feel good.

One day, PFC Spoon, our platoon medic and my best buddy, was sitting nearby. He opened his mail. The letter from his wife was only one short paragraph. He took a deep breath and swallowed. "My wife is pregnant for another man." Tears filled his eyes. "I love her. I need her. What did I do? What can I do? Life ain't worth living without her." Tears were pouring down his face. "I can't make it without her," he screamed and fell to his knees. His screams turned to moans and groans. A medical evacuation helicopter was called to take him back to Long Binh hospital, followed by transportation to a psychiatric hospital back in the States. I picked up Spoon's letter and read it before stuffing it in my rucksack.

The Bunker Line, Vietnam, 1968

Before I went to Vietnam, I had spent nine months in West Germany pulling guard duty on the Czechoslovakian border. While there, I had saved about $10,000 by operating a high-interest illegal lending business in the basement of my barracks. I also sold expensive shots of alcohol to soldiers in my military unit, and cut hair and sold German sausage to veterans who got hungry late at night. I was planning to use my savings after my return from Vietnam to start a family.

When I went home for two weeks before going to Vietnam, I deposited my savings in a bank account. Because of my mother's addiction to alcohol, I had doubts about her managing my finances but she convinced me she would take care for my money while I was away. Reluctantly, I placed her name on my account.

My two-week leave was great for me and my girlfriend. We vowed to love each other unconditionally while we were apart.

It was a bright, sunny day when the airplane wheels touched down on American soil. Taxiing down the runway seemed to take forever. The plane finally came to a stop some distance from International Arrivals. A soft voice announced, "Welcome home! Thanks for your service to our country." The door opened, and fresh air rushed in. It had been a year since I had breathed American air. Back in Vietnam the smell of Buddhist incense blended with the odors of death were a constant reminder of what I missed back home. I was eager to disembark and begin my 1,800-mile journey home.

With mud on my boots from my last patrol and sweat dried into my jungle fatigues, I made my way to the plane's exit. Briefly, I was overcome with emotion, but like a good soldier I stood erect, shoulders back, chin up. As the sun followed me down the stairs into the terminal for processing, my mind drifted back to the friends I left in Vietnam. Happiness abruptly turned to sadness. I could hear military personnel shouting orders, "Move it! Move up! Move it, soldiers! Pick it up!" I felt like I did not belong where I was at that moment and time. After clearing customs, I moved through the processing line, was fitted and given a dress military uniform, which consisted of black shoes, black socks, dress green shirt, black tie, and dress cap. I dressed and loaded onto a transportation bus to San Francisco International Airport. I held tightly to my orders, which included my ticket home.

We crossed over the Bay Bridge headed for the airport, and I began to cheer up as the bus pulled up to the terminal. I rushed inside, got my seat assignment, and headed to the gate. I located a seat in the airport waiting area that allowed me to sit in a defensive position. People were everywhere; fear and paranoia pushed my sense of reality to the limit. I struggled to control my feelings. A white man sat down next to me. "Nigger," he said, "what are you doing in an American soldier's uniform? It's for white men only, boy." I lost control and a violent altercation ensued.

Airport security came and tore my fingers from around his neck. I was handcuffed and taken to a holding room. Several hours later, a military officer arrived. I was released to his custody and escorted to a waiting plane home. He wished me well. I saluted, placed my duffle bag over my shoulder, and headed for the plane. The airline steward greeted me with a smile as I entered the plane. I sat next to a clergyman who was holding a cross between his fingers. His eyes were closed. I buckled my seat belt and said a long prayer. The plane taxied down the runway for takeoff while I was praying. My mind drifted from prayers to being back home in church. I realized I didn't pray a lot in Vietnam. The war had left me without faith in God or church. I could hear the landing gear locking the wheels into the fuselage of the plane. The incident back at the San Francisco airport had left me wondering what to expect when I arrived back home. Everything had been legally segregated when I had left. I asked myself, could I take that now? After putting my life on the line for my country, would I be able to turn my head and walk away from insults? I pushed my seat back, closed my eyes, and drifted off to sleep.

Turbulence shook the plane, and I woke from a nightmare. I thought I was trapped in a bunker in Vietnam. I could see PFC Spoon on his knees crying profusely about a letter from home. I saw bombs falling from B-52 aircraft and felt the ground shaking beneath me. Rockets from Viet Cong positions flashed before me, and I thought leaches were hanging from my genitals after a fire fight in the Delta mud. A flight attendant with an arm full of small pillows asked if I was OK. I composed myself and nodded.

Vietnam, Base Camp, Son Bay, 1969

The clergyman sitting next to me asked if I wanted him to pray for me. I insisted that my faith in God was lost in Vietnam. "No one gets to heaven except though the Son who died on the cross," he said. I told him part of me died in Vietnam. He said, "God puts us through hardships and struggle, then he uses us to do his will." I never had a white man minister to me because all of our churches were segregated back home. But I think I needed to hear his words. I couldn't understand what was happening to me. Before the war, I was quiet and caring. Nothing in my small-town upbringing helped me understand this emotional change. Turbulence shook the plane again, harder than before. I called the Lord's name. Fear of a plane crash crossed my mind. I asked myself, how could the plane go down so close to home after I escaped death so many times in the jungles of Vietnam? The minister and I began to pray together; tears streamed down my cheeks. The flight attendant appeared with lunch in her hands. I thanked the minister for praying with me and lowered the tray attached to the back of the seat in time for the small meal of chicken, roll, salad, and two cookies.

After we landed at Dallas-Fort Worth airport, I looked for a pay phone to call my girlfriend. I dialed her number and a few rings later, her mother answered. She said my girlfriend was at work. "Tell her I will be home in about three hours, please." She abruptly hung up the phone. She had treated me like a stranger and not the young man she had wanted her daughter to marry a year ago. Dismayed, I made it to the departure gate.

The phone call to my girlfriend left me feeling uneasy. Tension filled my body as the plane moved away from the gate onto the runway behind a succession of planes headed for takeoff. I realized I was no longer in combat mode, and I didn't have a buddy support system around me. My buddies were back in Vietnam, and the world I was facing now required a different response than pulling the trigger on an M-16 rifle or detonating a claymore mine, or pulling the pin on a hand grenade, or inserting a blasting cap into C-4 plastic explosives.

The small propeller-driven plane bounced and dipped its way toward Shreveport. After 45 minutes, the pilot announced, "Attendants, prepare the cabin for landing." The wheels touched down, and I was overcome with emotions as the plane stopped at the terminal. Night had fallen over this small-town airport. One baggage handler was on duty. He placed the passengers' luggage on an old, wooden table under a metal roof.

I grabbed my duffle bag and got into a rundown cab that carried me to the Trailways bus station, arriving just in time to catch the last bus home. I paid the cab driver, jumped out, and rushed to the waiting bus. The bus driver checked my military travel voucher. I took my seat, and the luggage compartment door was slammed shut. For a moment, the slammed baggage compartment door reminded me of an explosion and firefight in Vietnam. I did not know I was suffering from post traumatic stress disorder, an illness suffered by combat soldiers who had endured war.

I had written my mother and girlfriend informing them of my arrival on March 20. I had so much to look forward to, yet I was doubtful. I put my head in my hands and said a prayer. The bus pulled away from the terminal. Dimly lit streets were sparse with traffic as we sped south via Highway One to Natchitoches.

Coming home left me filled with trepidation about where my place in society would be. I had been physically liberated in Vietnam while my mind remained in psychological prison, resulting from growing up in a segregated environment that limited opportunities in the use of schools, restrooms, restaurants, and employment, where it was illegal to vote and socialize freely.

Lights from the bus flashed on a sign that read, "You are entering Powhatan, Louisiana," a small village sixteen miles from home and the ancestral home of four generations of my family. I started thinking about my mother's home cooking: neck bones, rice, red beans, corn bread, and lots of hot sauce. My girlfriend would be waiting at mama's house as she always did. I had purchased an engagement ring in Singapore while on R&R. I thought we loved each other, and I believed getting married would stop this emotional roller coaster I was on. I thought it was just the right medicine I needed to get back to my old self. The driver pulled up to the station and stopped. He opened the door and hurried to the baggage compartment. I trailed close behind him. He opened it up, and I pulled out my duffle bag. I was the only passenger getting off who was dressed in an army uniform.

Vietnam, Ready for Eagle Flight, 1968

My brother drove up as the bus pulled away. I was surprised. He was not known for doing good deeds for me. I threw my duffle bag into the back of his truck. He showed no outward emotions and was not particularly excited to see me. The ride to mama's house was short. The streets were quiet; no cheering crowds welcomed my arrival. Motion picture newsreels of veterans marching down Fifth Avenue in New York crossed my mind. They had received a hero's welcome. We arrived at mama's, and I saw her standing in the doorway. She rushed to meet the truck. I jumped out and embraced her. My tears streamed onto her face. We made our way back into the house. My sister was waiting with her husband. Suddenly and without warning, I became fearful and anxious; I backed into a back bedroom of the house. My sister called out and said they would see me the next day. I didn't answer. I felt paralyzed by fear. My brother asked what was wrong. I told him, I didn't know, but I would be OK. After a short rest sitting on the side of the bed, I lay down and closed my eyes, but could not sleep. Then I lay on the floor behind the bed thinking I would feel safer. I got up and shut the door and pushed the dresser against it. I didn't sleep well the first night I was at home. I awakened several times, and my body was soaking with sweat. The nightmares had tired me out. I felt like I had walked through jungle terrain with a heavy rucksack on my back.

Daylight began to creep through the window; roosters were starting to crow. I could hear mama moving around in the kitchen. I smelled the odor of strong black coffee. I got up dreading having to use the outdoor toilet in our backyard, the same one I grew up with. Mama opened the back door to the kitchen and said, "Breakfast is almost ready." My visit to the outdoor toilet was quick. I stopped to wash my hands at an outdoor water faucet with a piece of lye soap before sitting down to eat.

Mama joined me at the table. She stared at me a lot and seemed to be uncomfortable with my presence. The ham, eggs, grits, and butter-filled biscuits were good. She asked me how long I would be home, and I told her I had sixteen days but would leave in ten since I planned to drive to Fort Lewis in Washington State where I would finish up my tour of duty. She asked if I planned to get married. I said yes. "You will need money for a car and a wife. And you won't be able to help take care of me if you get married," she said. I told her I would always help her as much as I could once I settled into a good job.

"You could come home and add to the back of this house and move your family right here with me."

"Mama, I sent you $10,000 to save for me. I told you before I left for Vietnam, I wanted to buy a new car and make a down payment on a house once I got married."

My mother seemed irritated, and she stood up and walked back into her room. I heard her old dresser drawer open and shut. She returned to the kitchen and threw a small, black, bank book on the table. She said, "That's what's left in your savings." I opened the bank book; it read $76.10. I screamed and screamed, "How could you spend all of my money? How could you do this to me?"

"You owed me for putting up with your ass all these years," she said. "I sacrificed every day of my life for you. I am your mother, and you want to give your money to some no-good young bitch. I taught you, cooked for you, kept a roof over your head." I took a deep breath trying to compose myself. "Mama, it ain't right what you have done. I helped where I could in this house all my life. I did what was asked of me. When I made money, I gave you more than half. I did everything to be a good son."

Tears dripped from my chin. The energy was drained from my body, knowing all of my money had been spent. I pulled myself together enough to get to the phone in the living room to call my girlfriend. Someone answered the phone and hung it up. I didn't know what to think or feel. I was confused, and fear gripped my body.

My mother came into the living room and reminded me that the phone I was using cost money and the food that I had eaten was not cheap. For a few minutes, thoughts of killing my mother occupied my mind. I withdrew to the back bedroom. Once there, tears streamed down my face. I lay across the bed until it was almost dark.

My girlfriend lived on the east side of town. I called an old high school friend who lived down the street from her to come pick me up. He came right over. We were happy to see each other. We talked about old times on our way to her house. We arrived at my girlfriend's mother's home and stopped near the front entrance. Lights were on in the living room. I could see the love of my life sitting on a sofa near an unknown man. My heart was pounding so hard. My friend told me to stay calm. Uncertainty turned to anger. I opened the car door, stepped out, and slammed it shut. It must have spooked her; she rushed to the screen door and looked out. I made my way up the three stairs leading to the porch. I was overwhelmed. Things seem to be in slow motion.

The woman I had been in love with since I was a teenager was standing there. I reached for her; she stepped back into the house and gestured with her hand toward an empty sofa. She sat back down with her arm around the man in her living room. I was too choked up to speak. Anger turned to grief. I forced myself to look in the eyes of the woman I thought a year ago would become my wife. After a few minutes, I stood and asked her what I did wrong. "I got lonely after you left for Vietnam," she said. I wanted to lash out violently, but I loved her too much. I retreated to the door, turned and wished her all the best. I was weak in my knees, and it was difficult to go down the stairs. I knew our relationship was over.

Looking beyond this painful event in my life seemed impossible. In the car, my buddy tried to calm me down. I began to hyperventilate. My stress level was unbearable. We were seventy miles from the nearest Veterans Hospital in Shreveport. I was deteriorating mentally, and he drove as fast as he could to get there. Forty minutes later, he pulled into emergency entrance of hospital. Emergency personnel removed me from the car and placed me on a stretcher. They kept me overnight on the psychiatric floor and discharged me with a large bottle of Valium, a drug used to treat depression in veterans at that time.

I returned home from the hospital on a Trailways bus that day disillusioned, with thoughts of committing suicide racing through my mind. Coming home was supposed to be a happy occasion after surviving a war. I was a young man, and I didn't know love was not forever or that trusting someone with my life savings would destroy my faith in humanity.

I made it back to my mother's house. As I entered the front door, we made eye contact. I continued to the back room where I packed my duffle bag and prepared to leave for my next assignment at Fort Lewis, Washington.

The next day, I took one Valium and lay in bed. I was awakened by a knock at my window. My girlfriend had sent my best buddy to bring me to her home. I was suspicious about her intentions, but love is strange. A flicker of light in the dark corner of my heart still reminded me how much I loved her. With my spirit broken and needing something or someone to hold onto, I reluctantly agreed to ride to her house. I had slept until nearly 11:30 P.M. We arrived at her place at about midnight.

She was waiting in the doorway dressed in a thin, white, loosely fitting, knee-high gown. Excited, I rushed up the stairs and slid my fingers inside the open gown and gently around her smooth brown waist and drew her as close as I could to the erection in my pants. I briefly lost track of time. I pushed my tongue as far as I could into her mouth. She led me to a sofa and turned off an overhead light. I removed my pants and underwear in one downward motion. I used my toes to pin my pants leg to the floor and free my feet. She spread her nude body out on the sofa. I laid my body into her waiting arms. After our intercourse, I was without emotion or pity because I knew another man was in her life. Thoughts of killing her entered my mind for the pain she had caused me, yet I was satisfied that this is what it took to put this chapter of my life behind me.

I dressed and held her close, kissed her, looked into her eyes, and walked away. The next day, I woke early, ate breakfast, and took a Valium. I dressed in full military attire for my trip to Washington. The neighbor next door had offered to take me to the airport in Shreveport. I slung my duffle bag over my shoulder realizing I would not be back soon. My mother was asleep as I walked past her bed on my way out the door. I had not learned enough about forgiveness to forgive her at that time. I locked the door and left.

Eight hours later, I arrived at Fort Lewis. For the first few months at the base, I struggled with depression, startled responses in public, hypervigilance, anger, and constant fear of the unknown. I was placed in the Veteran's Hospital psychiatric ward and treated for trauma. I will never forget the feeling when I saw PFC Spoon walk in my room one day. It was one of the greatest feelings in my life just to realize we had survived. I reached into my overnight bag and handed Spoon the Dear John letter he had received while in Vietnam. He smiled and said, "It's all behind me now." I continued to be involved in the Veteran's Hospital Post Traumatic Stress Disorder clinic for twenty years.

Nine months later my girlfriend had our child. Sadly, my girlfriend has spent most of her years since in a psychiatric hospital. I have had intermittent contact with our daughter, who has grown into a talented, educated woman.

After my discharge from the Army, I excelled at various jobs. In 1980, my mother suffered a debilitating stroke that paralyzed one side of her body. I returned home and was at her bedside for the last two months of her life, caring for her the best that I could. One day while she was lying in the hospital, we made peace. I told her I loved her and always would.

Today, I am happily married, the father of four children who are all very happy adults. Though I live daily with chronic pain, I am only better off because my buddy in Vietnam took a bullet meant for me. I never forgot the prayer with the minister on the plane. My wife and I attend church regularly. God has blessed me in this life with more than I ever would have imagined.

My art is a life-sustaining part of my existence and has given me mental and emotional support through many struggles. It helped me survive the dark days of lingering poverty and at the same time allowed me to lift myself up beyond the pale of ignorance by visualizing and articulating in two- and three-dimensional compositions.

The stories and art in this book express life among common people along Cane River farms and small towns who picked cotton and used their creative talents in labor and trades to foster self-esteem and hope for a better tomorrow. In my world travels, I have found that self preservation is a universal language that I have been blessed to express in words and art.

A Journey

(Dedicated to my daughter Kheysia)

Love given too late
Has come to say
The little seed grew
Between the two
Deep down through
Into a single belonging
A life begotten
A life grew
Spreading pinnacles of love
A warm love
The first love
Remembered
Love given, in time
Grows to last
Fertility's first love drop
A beginning that has never stopped
Asleep it grows
Touching shades and colors
Reaching for unconquered hearts
Love is always traveling near

The Sculpture Series
1986–2012

Roosevelt Lewis in his sculpting studio, 2012   Photograph by Lisa Brown

On Sculpting

Curling my fingers around a wood chisel gives me great satisfaction. By the time I lay a well-seasoned piece of rough wood between my vises, the visual aspects of how I will approach a piece had begun months, even years, before.

It is like a spiritual baptism without immersion in water for me.

Sculpting takes place when pressure is applied to an even-tempered swing of a wood mallet, when it hits the butt of a chisel. After years of carving, focus on the process comes naturally. As the extracted wood piles up around my feet and patience turns to pleasure, the sight of an emerging piece of art is rewarding.

I use a variety of wood colors to achieve my goal, and I use eight to twelve sculpting tools, varying in shape and size, to bring character and life to a finished work.

When the texture and wood grain reveal themselves, I am in touch with something sacred.

Generations

Poplar
42½" x 7" x 10"
2008

Corner Boy

Clear lacquer on cedar
17" x 5" x 6½"
2003

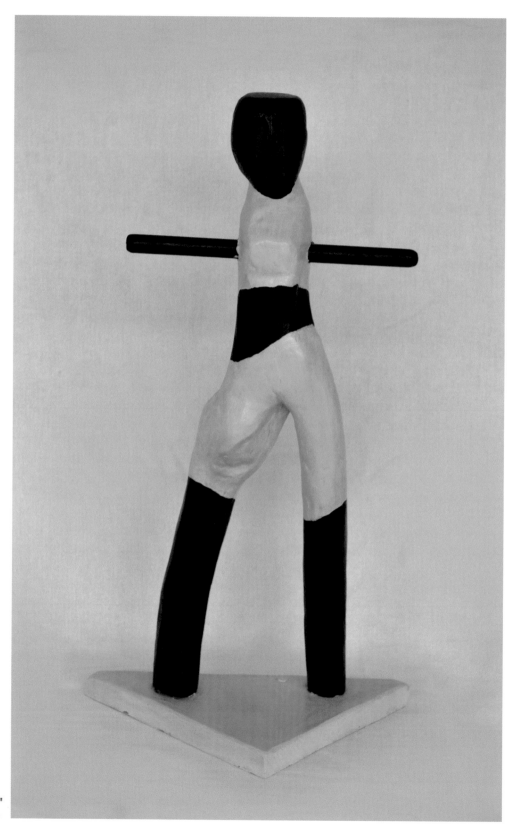

Untitled (1986)

Acrylic on apple
18" x 10"
1986

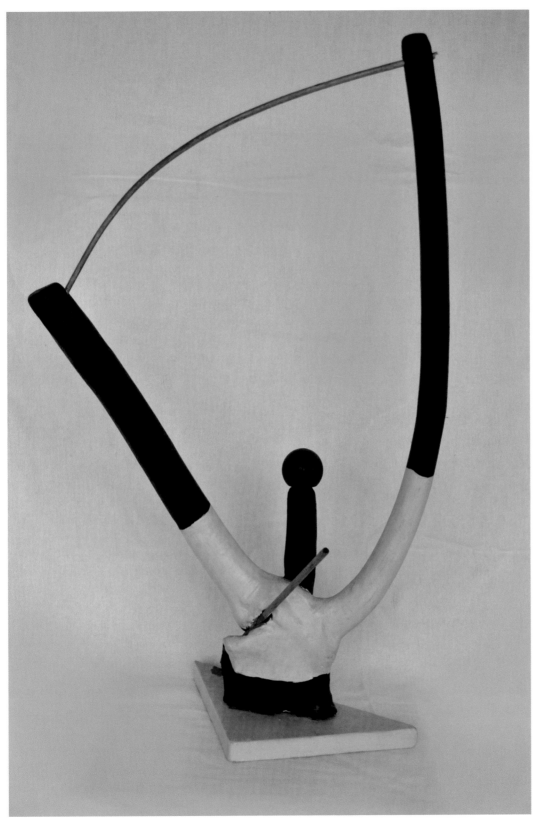

Blood Spear

Acrylic on apple
24" x 14½"
1986

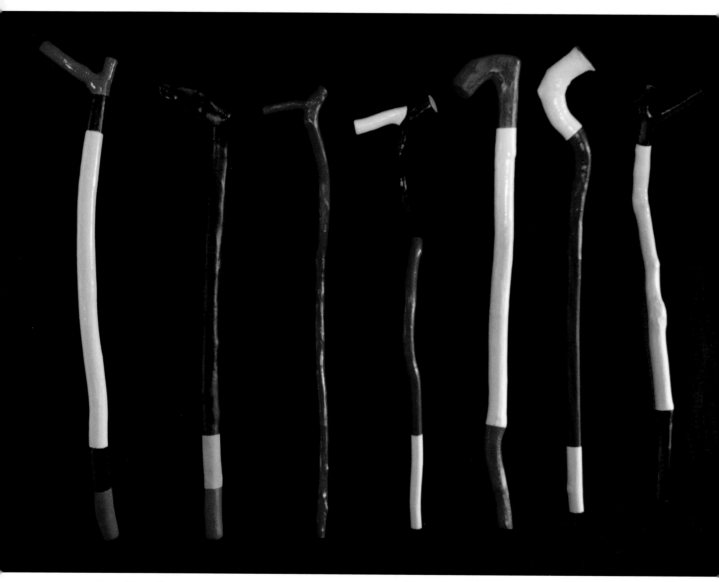

Cane River Canes

Acrylic on apple
37" to 38"
1988 through 2000

Out of Africa

Acrylic on maple
23½" x 11½" x ¾"
1988

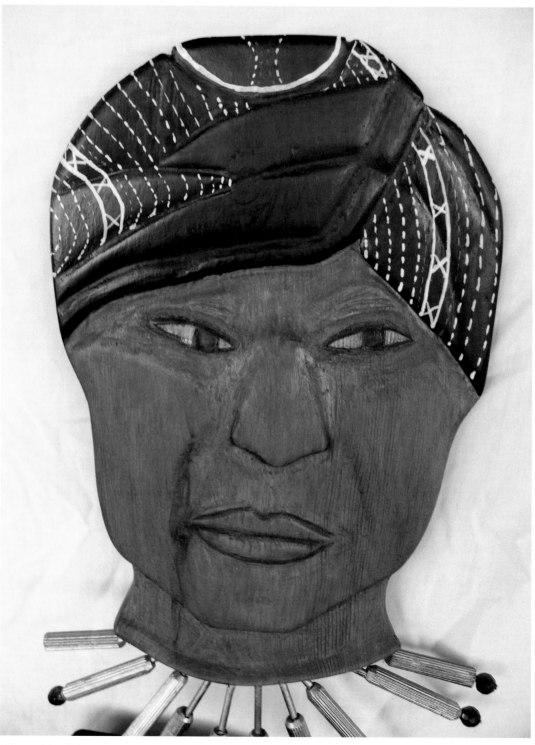

Winnie Mandela

Acrylic on maple
17" x 9" x ¾"
1988

Angry Lady

Acrylic on maple
17½" x 9½" x 4"
1988

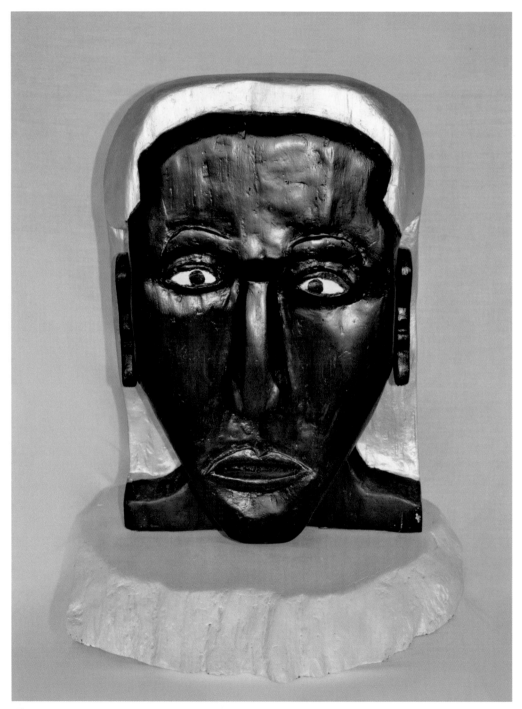

African Queen

Acrylic on maple
13½" x 16" x 14"
1988

New Birth

Acrylic on mahogany
25" x 11" x 1"
1989

Abstract Lady

Acrylic on walnut
22" x 11" x 3"
1990

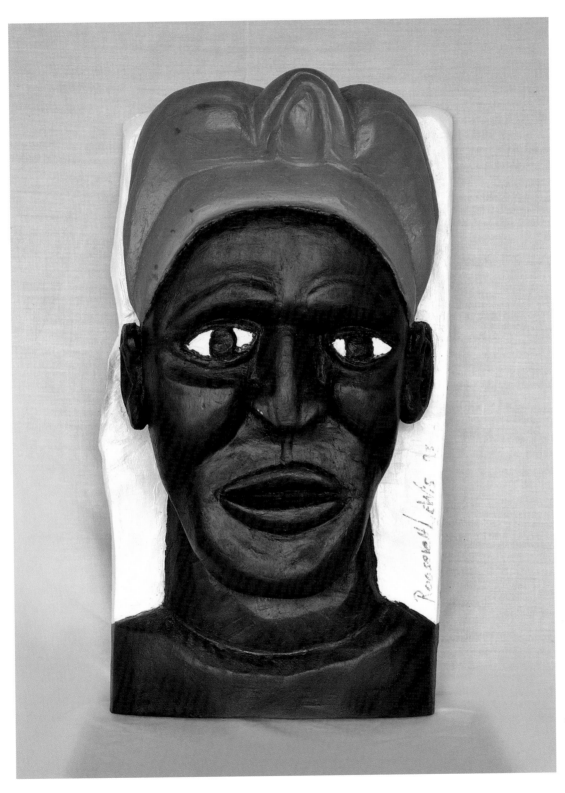

African Chief

Acrylic on walnut
17" x 10" x 5½"
1993

Kenyon Tribesman

Ebony
10" x 5" x 5"
2002

Homeless Man

Clear lacquer over
acrylic on cedar
23½" x 8" x 6½"
2003

Love Tree

Walnut
24" x 15½" x 7¼"
2000

Ethiopian Woman

Alaskan fir with
burlap and seashells
23½" x 11½" x 3½"
1986

The Paintings
1987–2012

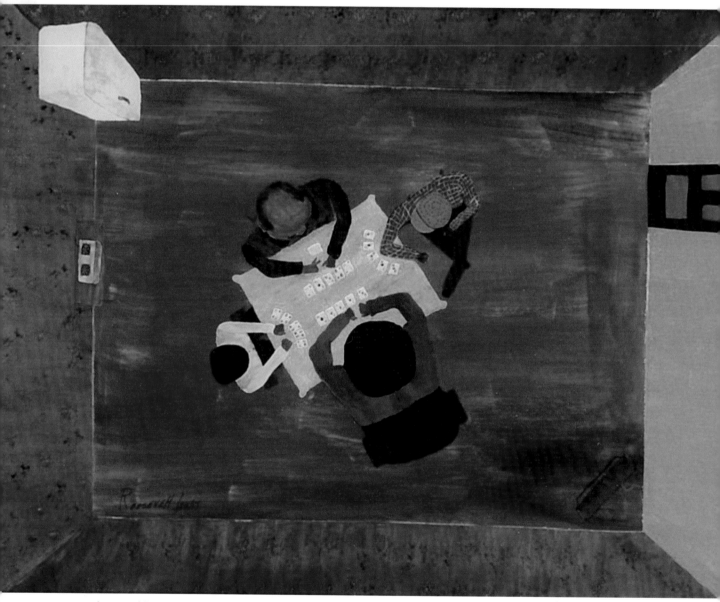

The Gambling Shack

Acrylic on paper
30" x 20"
1988

Mrs. Hazel

Acrylic on illustration board
32½" x 39"
1987

Tribute to Dr. King

Acrylic on canvas
48" x 24"
1989

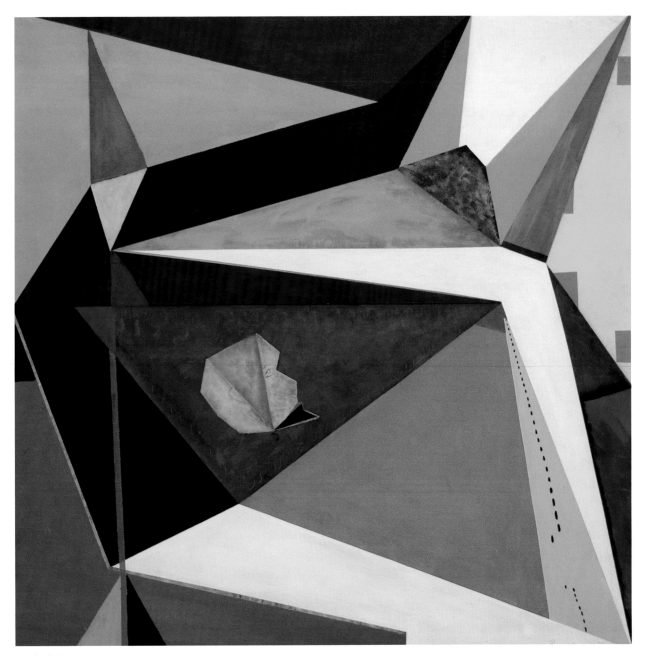

Invictious

Acrylic on canvas
48" x 48"
1988

Untitled (1990)

Acrylic on canvas
52½" x 30¼"
1990

Cajun Lady Dancing

Acrylic on paper
23" x 19"
1996

Nevaeh

Acrylic on canvas
48" x 48"
1996

Devil in a Red Dress

Acrylic on paper
16" x 23"
1997

Godmother

Acrylic on illustration board
20" x 15"
1997

Mother Holding Baby

Acrylic on illustration board
40" x 33¾"
2007

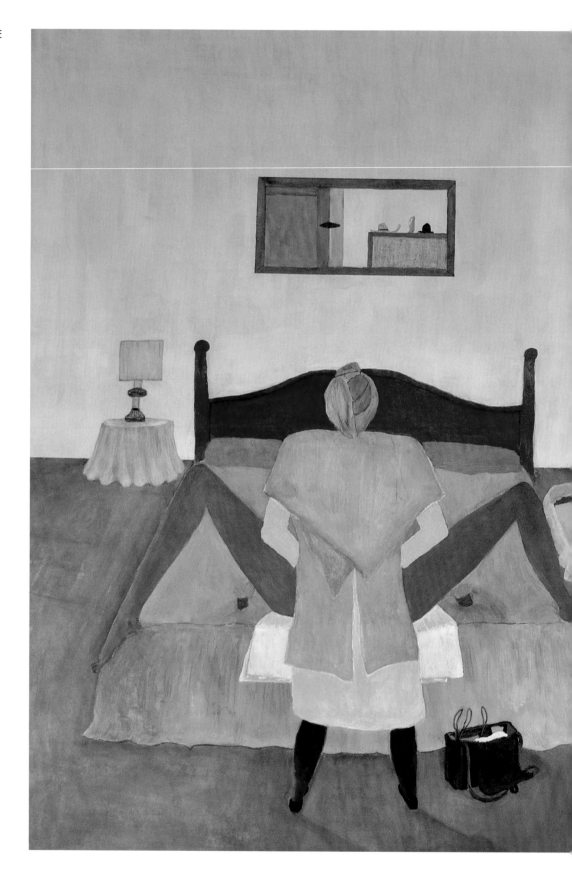

Midwife

Acrylic on illustration board
35" x 29"
2006

Lying on the Street

Lying on the street
Destination back alleys and Main Street
Another cold, rainy, and wet sleep
Sounds of the early morning ritual of the garbage truck
The garbage man

Another dent in another can
Echoes ring in my brain
While lying and waiting
The rain stopped
The garbage can is empty
And the hunger pains are a cold, empty plate

Now—the morning brings footsteps
Bright shiny shoes stepping into
The bright morning light—with this
Rain and wind brought
Sunshine slowly piercing through
A brick skyline

Shadows from the buildings move with time
Shiny shoes tiptoe around the wet wintery walkway
They thump their cigarette butts down
The city drains while waiting for a light to change
—lying on the street
Clutching the green, empty bottle of slow death

Lying on the street finding strength enough
To ask and reach and then be called
A street leech
Here down on your luck
With nothing but a thrown-away cigarette butt
Lying, watching footsteps—slowly sleep has its way

It's night again; hope appears in the eyes of the hungry
—sounds in the alley are sounds
Of an angry dishwasher dumping garbage
From a steam-filled doorway

Lying here the body feels good knowing
Trash to others is strength to
Frail hands reaching inside a can
Dreams faded—but hopes for a warmer winter
A longer summer—prayer answered
From long ago

New Orleans After the Storm

Acrylic on illustration board
32½" x 42½"
2003

Doors of No Return

Acrylic on illustration board
43" x 32¾"
2002

Bloody Caddo

Acrylic on illustration board
43" x 31"
2011

The Moment

Acrylic on illustration board
48" x 48"
2000

The Spirit Covers the White House

Acrylic on illustration board
42½" x 32"
2009

Shades of Color

Acrylic on canvas
17½" x 48"
2007

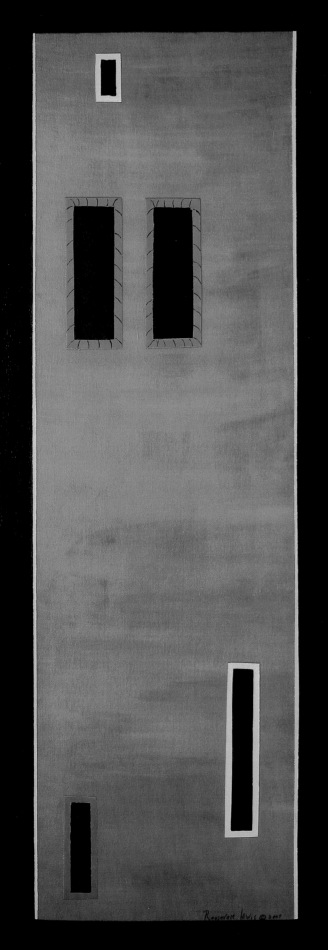

Untitled I
Acrylic on canvas
17½" x 48"2007

Untitled II

Acrylic on canvas
18 x 24"
2007

Untitled III

Acrylic on canvas
18" x 24"
2007

Trapped by Life

Acrylic on canvas
36" x 36"
2006

The Blood of Trayvon

Acrylic on illustration board
43" x 26"
2012

Abstract Natchitoches

Acrylic on canvas
48" x 24"
2002

Northwest master artists, from left:
Al Doggett, Ernest Thomas, Eric Salisbury, Hiawatha Davis, Roosevelt Lewis

Photograpy by Constance L. Thomas, 2013

Afterword

Art reflects life and is an essential contributor to how we come to see life and life's experiences. Artistic expression contextualizes our understanding of what we remember and what we ultimately do with the understanding of those memories as the inevitable questions are raised through our reflections.

In *Taught by Life: Art and Stories,* Roosevelt Lewis brings to life the incredible tapestry of a people's historic journey in a beautiful and poignant collection of stories and images.

The African American people during the beginning of the turn of the century in Louisiana had a significant and vibrant impact on the history, legacy, and collective cultural continuum in the United States of America. Lewis's poignant stories of tremendous challenge and resistance in the face of tumultuous times during the struggle for freedom and the pursuit of happiness speak volumes. They remind us all about the depth of human sacrifices made in those seminal and defining times and give us all an opportunity to engage, in a very visceral and personal way, with our own history.

The stories shared in Lewis's wonderful autobiographical, pictorial book take us on an incredible journey and will invite many to open up courageous conversations around the proverbial table of dialogue.

Kudos to Roosevelt Lewis for his beautiful contribution to the continuing and enduring revelation of the African American journey and the formative role it has played in the American story and legacy.

— Tawnya Pettiford-Wates, PhD
Associate Professor, Theatre Department
Virginia Commonwealth University

Founder & Artistic Director
The Conciliation Project

Works of Art

in chronological order